M000251829

ADVANCED PRAISE FOR **SOFT BOY.**

For more information contact:
David A. Gaines
http://www.davegpoetry.com

for my family & every boy i love.

Audiences know what to expect,
& that is all that they are prepared to believe in.
—Tom Stoppard

love is an action, never simply a feeling.
—bell hooks

AFFIRMATION SLIP.

i, _____ (name), give myself permission to be present.
i understand we are going on a field trip; that i will be driving this bus, &
the stories herein, for as long as i choose to stay. i agree to travel at my own
pace & take necessary breaks. i acknowledge there is no destination; that
any & all conclusions i arrive at through this journey are my own invention.
i accept that my thoughts, feelings & healing are my sole responsibility.

_____   _____
signature   date

poems by david a. gaines

SEATING ARRANGEMENT

DA RULES.

alright alright everybody listen up settle down i'm required to read these
rules to you before we pull off & i hate repeating myself & i hate myself so
if i have to hear me twice that's gon be your ass now

- ☐ no eating
- ☐ no drinking
- ☐ no punching

unless he deserves it we not making any stops so if you need to use the
bathroom do it now or forever hold your piss yo i said *shut the fuck up*
if i gotta come back there again yo ass walking home okay

- ☐ no loud music
- ☐ no loud anything
- ☐ no switching seats

stay where you been assigned at birth don't put anything out the window
not yo head not yo hands not yo feet not yo sense of self we need all of that
also
- ☐ no buddy system—every man for himself
- ☐ if you get lost—don't get lost
- ☐ if you have an emergency—don't have an emergency

pretty simple ay phones away while i'm talking that's ya'll problem today
always distracted never paying attention to where you're going last year
this boy stepped off the bus without looking & fell & just kept falling & we
ain't seen him since

now i'll be coming around to collect permission slips if you don't have one
that's okay ya'll forged the signatures like your genders anyway it's all good
we all headed to the same place

i bet y'all wondering where we're going well that's for me to know & for
you to find out after we get there all you need to know is we gon make a
man out of you or you'll die trying

THE ELEPHANT & THE TAMER.

"when the elephant was young, the wise tamer fastened a thin rope around the calf's leg so no matter how hard he thrashed for freedom he could not escape. when the calf grew into an adult, stocked with hulking trunk & legs thick as redwood trees, all the tamer needed was a rope & the giant would yield to his captivity."

my father loves to tell this story.
each time he lauds the poacher.
his smile lingers like a noose.
& he says he's proud
to have made me
a man.

GENESIS.

in the beginning
my first word
was "hallelujah"
which means
church baby, tongue
knows praise better
than his mama's name.

then God said, let us make man in our image
& i look just like my daddy,
the handsome preacher
whose lies became gospel.

after my father embezzles
my heart is no pipe organ
but it fills me with music,
leads a congregation of bones
into worship each time i rise.

after eighteen years of Communion Sundays
if i consume anymore of Jesus's flesh & blood
i might regurgitate him
back to life.

before rest, on the last day
i pray my death be a swift benediction.
this body, my first church
& life, the longest Sunday service.

don't let them say i was raised in church.
tell them i was the church
& *it was good.*

BIRTHDAY WISHES (I).

July 22
will make another year
since my baby sister drew

her last breath.
she was an artist.
two years old

& 28 pounds of poetry
with barely enough trust in her legs
to walk across the kitchen floor

but enough pride
in her palms to wipe my kisses
off her cheek.

her name is A███████
           but we call her A██████

██████ Gaines, 2, lived in this house on 69th Avenue in West Oak Lane

6

Tot left in car dies

she was forgotten in the car
after a late church service
on a scorching summer night

& found on the morning
of my third birthday.

which taught me:
not all birthday wishes come true.

but still, i wish
i could remember her.
maybe then grieving

wouldn't feel like chasing
runaway balloons.
if i catch them

i can miss her,
i can blow out the trick candle guilt
that returns every year.

we celebrate my birthday
on the beaches of Ocean City, MD.

i bury   my toes in the sand.
i soak under the same sun
that drowned her.

& they sing
happy   birthday
as if those two words fit together.

RITE OF PASSAGE.

my first haircut is a christening. a choir of clipper *hummmms* as ███████ carves sharp new boundaries into my virgin skin. i don't cry & daddy is proud. when i return home momma will say i look like a new man. & this my first lesson in sacrifice:

i'm defined by what i leave behind. be it the pruned strands gathered at the chair's feet or the version of me shed on the doorstep. here i'm a man unlike myself. fresh offering to a tender headed God.

i watch ragged men congregate inside the shop's belly, anticipating their turn to feel the cutting grace of our biweekly father. some temper this limbo with the bootleg movies playing for what feels like eternity; or the on-schedule entrance of a merchant selling more goods—scented oils, socks & shirts with logo horses not indigenous to their fabrics

while other men gossip comfortably in the de facto segregation of a barbershop on Saturday. one man suggests God gave him all daughters as some form of karma for a life of misogyny. & i wonder what kind of God would punish children with a father incapable of loving them.

a divine looking woman saunters past the window & the entire shop halts to stare. my daddy shouts *damn boy if i wasn't married!* as if he ain't more worried about his hairline leaving him than his wife. he flirts with women everywhere we go. but i've never seen him let another man touch his fade. & this my first lesson in faithfulness:

my chief loyalty is to my appearance in the eyes of men.

WRESTLING WASN'T FAKE IN 2008.

it was real as the star-freckled night sky
           or the hush over the bedroom of a boy

dodging his bedtime like conscription.
           it was real as the difference between boys

& men. i am still one pretending to be
           the other & this is its own reckless art.

on Friday nights i mold muses from men
           dressed in spandex & sweat & whatever

sweet glory glazes the body when a crowd
           savors the taste of your name in their mouths.

& i leap from the ropes of my lofty top bunk
           until the crashing summons my father's wrath.

some still name this violent miracle   *a hoax*
           but is it any less scripted than the world outside the ring?

every day i watch masked men & women
        suspend their disbelief in the name of a binary.

when my mother reflects on her broken marriage
        she remembers acting more feminine

so my father didn't feel *challenged*.
        i start dating   & join the chivalrous cast.

i open every door;   i pull out every chair.
        i pay for every meal until my wallet taps out.

i drop her off home & know my role is to make a move
        but the only moves i know are pile drivers

& holds to fashion submission. & no wonder i am still desperate
        for something to believe in that isn't for show.

THE SHOW MUST GO ON.

an acting teacher told me
the worst thing an actor can do
is break   character.

in high school i punched a boy
to impress some other boys.

i earned their respect.
a pitiful wage.

i heard the boy cried
himself to sleep that night.
how jealous i am of his fatigue.

vulnerability is a dangerous stunt.
to project is to make a double
out of someone.

i don't know how to cry
so i made him do it for me.

i'm even violent in my sleep.
i toss & turn. i jolt & kick.

but what man hasn't spent
a dark night heavy & restless

under the weight of a role?
i was cast at birth.

my mother says   *it's a boy*
my father sharpens his knives

carves my family
like a crescent moon.

i once drove 20 miles
in the wrong direction
despite realizing it after the first 10.

i couldn't accept my mistake
so i just kept going.

the greater the loss
the tighter the grip on what's left.

every man is a graveyard
of stifled hurt & buried emotion

so there will always be
more skeletons than men
who admit to making them.

i memorized the gendered script,
auditioned as a real man
& became understudy.

in my relationships
i want to wear the pants
but they're highwaters.

i feel feminine
in all the wrong places.

i'm not afraid of being afraid
but i fear who i am if i'm not feared.

my friends label me *non-threatening*
& i swallow the compliment

despite it sitting in my stomach
like a sour treason.

there i go again typecasting myself
—always playing the victim.

there is no applause
for what must be done.

some weeks after i made a boy weep
i walked into my study hall

& another boy fixed his gaze on me.
when it lingered past comfort

i asked   *is there something in my teeth?*
he replied   *my fist if you disrespect me again.*

& threatened me every time
we crossed paths for months.

i know he didn't really want to hurt me.
he just wanted me
to   break.

WHEN YOU STEP ON A FRESH PAIR OF JORDANS.

their owner / will threaten to kill you. / not for the misplaced heel. / you can't unmake a stain / but if he can turn you into one / it'll ease the ache / of knowing everything he loves / can be ruined in an instant. / i mean we all got niggas / who lost their freedom / stepping on the toes / of someone with the power / to only wear sneakers by choice. / & you can say sorry / but apologies won't bring ▮▮▮▮home / or help his daughter / pick out her shoes / for school today. / & haven't you also found warmth / in this ice veined country / by fighting / small, winnable battles? / we all coping with some shit / we couldn't control. / so when their owner asks you / to repent / for having feet. / only ever apologize / for forgetting / where you left them.

MAN ON A MISSION.

as a boy i thought Apollo 13 was staged.   what is more unbelievable
than a man   admitting he has a problem?   they say
outer space is a sprawling   void   where no one can hear you
scream.   friendships with men are no different.   my nigga
lost his grandmother   at the speed of headlights.   an oblivious driver
crashed into her celestial body   like a brazen meteor   & now they
are worlds   apart.   i call my nigga & he sighs
the breath of a son   collapsing into himself.   i want to tell him—
          i know how it feels to be lost inside grief's orbit.
                    but all our manhood will permit is
               ay ▮▮▮▮ still searching through your phone?
he doesn't listen   when i critique his infidelity.   what good is logic
to a man   with his head above the clouds?   if he prefers
looking down   he'll believe   what doesn't challenge him
     back to earth.   dissociation isn't rocket science.
     when our bodies are present   & our hearts stranded
we are truly as invincible   as our fathers forged us to be.
as boys we learned   to alienate our feelings.   it's easier to
imagine   we are not from this planet   than it is to accept
what we've done   to ourselves   & to those who love us
          too much to be distant.   life   is a miserable trek.
     the loneliest travelers   never make it home.

18

THE STRANGER.

i have mastered the vile
art of estranging myself
in the name of pleasure
or duty   or fear
of what a mirror might say
in my company.

i'll barter my reflection
to whatever voiceless thrill
won't surface the iceberg
beneath my sunken eyes.

as a child i was afraid
to be alone & i still am.

i outgrew my clothes
but not my coping mechanisms
& ain't that just how it goes?

my last lover left me, said
i was never   *there*
& no wonder our year together
felt more like a few short weeks

like i just woke up one day
& she was a fresh absence.

i know it's still a breakup
even if i left myself first.

i know i'm speaking
of something grander
than loneliness.

what will a man endure
to circumvent the vulnerability
that intimacy demands?

SELF-IMMOLATION.

all the men in my life
proudly light themselves on fire
& say   *look at how dangerous i am*

SOFT BOY.

soft boy knows he's soft
but doesn't want you to think he's soft.

soft boy not like the other boys.
soft boy has feeeeeeeeelings

& no idea what to do with them.
soft boy loves his momma.

soft boy sensitive.
soft boy cries.

soft boy wears sweaters
& cuffs his jeans.

soft boy listens to Fleetwood Mac.
soft boy switches to Biggie around his niggas.

soft boy is terrible at sports
& being aggressive in general.

soft boy claims he ain't gay but feels
threatened around men more attractive than him.

soft boy cries.
soft boy reads books.

soft boy woke.
soft boy feminist.

soft boy says "free the nipple!"
so he can get a better view.

soft boy paints a picture of patriarchy
always landscape, never self-portrait.

soft boy wears a dress.
soft boy "reinventing masculinity"

or so soft boy says.
soft boy wolf in femme clothing.

soft boy evolved fuck boi.
soft boy cries.

soft boy likes your posts.
soft boy slides in your DMs, respectfully.

soft boy doesn't fuck.
soft boy "makes love."

soft boy loves to cuddle.
soft boy little spoon.

soft boy "doesn't believe in labels."
soft boy ghosts you.

soft boy sorry.
soft boy has been going through it.

soft boy makes you feel guilty.
soft boy cries.

soft boy victim.
soft boy cries.

soft boy cries.
soft boy cries.

soft boy working on himself.
soft boy trying his best.

soft boy thinks his efforts enough.
soft boy thinks his softness enough.

HYPOCRITES (EVERYONE I KNOW).

i know a pastor who drives a mercedes
& rents motels for his mistresses.

i know a brother who fasts religiously
but always feeds his ego.

i know a cousin who thinks contraception is evil
but never leaves his phone unprotected.

i know an uncle who believes "love thy neighbor"
doesn't extend to his gay son.

i know a father who blames the devil
for the consequences of his actions.

i know i'm no holier than thou.

i know i say i'm an open book
but the realest pages are torn out.

i know i told my lover i'd protect her
& didn't mean from me.

i know what i love & what i fear
are two sides of the same coin

& i always spend it on myself.

CHURCH&STATE.

separation   is only temporary   escape

i stopped going to church   despite my mother's invitations

a few months back   she asked me to pray over our meal

i respectfully declined   i replied *why didn't you divorce him sooner?*

she is all sanctuary & survival   she fled us to Texas to break free

my father only spoke in violence   like a hurricane   Harvey displaced

claimed victim(s)   & Lakewood kept its doors shut

& lied to protect public perception   seeing must be believing

my father found us in Texas   my mother staged a happy marriage

my mother reads bedtime stories   with knives hidden under the mattress

i kept waiting for him to change   she prays over her meal alone

i want to believe in their innocence   i want forgiveness to be enough

but power can't be destroyed   even when you don't know you have it

even if you take off the uniform   every cop i know goes to church when i say fuck 12, i mean

they are not God's elect

my father doesn't take no for an answer

i feel his presence even in his absence

is this a haunting? in high school

he threatened me

i lied bold in his face

he discovered the truth

my eye took weeks to heal

he says, never lie to him again

in his home

in an arbitrary pool

one derives authority

on their own time.

they are not the disciples

yet they claim a higher power

i ignore my father's calls

is this conditioning?

he caught me smoking weed

asked *where did you get this?*

no snitching

he punched me

i turned the other cheek

an off-duty officer killed a man

three years prior my father baptized me

i often wonder how

to introduce a person to God

BIRTHDAY WISHES (II).

i wish my family
wasn't afraid to say her name.

  Dead tot's kin won't talk

her birthday arrives
& our mouths shut
like tiny caskets.

DA: No charges in tot's death

so when asked,

how many siblings do you have?

i say   *two.*
i don't know how to say   *three.*

i'm scared to introduce her to strangers
when i feel like a stranger myself.

i wish that A
wasn't the reason my mother loves me
like she's afraid to lose another child.

growing up
she set so many rules
but her hugs were stricter.

i think she tries to cram me
into the hole left in her chest.

i think she hides tears in her palms
but momma, i see your fingers dripping.

i see her body in the bags
under your eyes.

i wish
we gave A███████
a safer nickname.

i wish
i could give my sister a better
hand-me-down than my birthday

but i'm too weak
to hand down anything
but this poem,

to make her real off paper
where there's nowhere
to hide.

i wish
every obituary didn't read: *In Loving Memory.*

memory isn't the only way
we keep our loved ones alive.

i'll remember A█████   *In Loving Poetry.*

i wish
i never had to write
this poem.

you know what they say
about wishes that are said
out loud.

THE RAPTURE: A BEDTIME STORY.

"ONCE UPON A TIME, THERE WAS NO TIME. THERE
WAS ONLY GOD, SEATED GOLD THRONE IN HEAVEN,
SURROUNDED BY ANGELS IN CEASELESS CELEBRATION.
THEY DANCED WITHOUT FATIGUE TO INSTRUMENTS YOU
CAN'T IMAGINE; SANG SONGS SO BEAUTIFUL & BREATHLESS
THEY'D COLLAPSE MORTAL LUNGS. BUT DESPITE THE WAY
THEIR VIBRANT GOWNS SHIMMERED IN THE ETERNAL
SUNSHINE, OR HOW MUCH WINE FLOODED THE YELLOW-
BRICK STREETS IN THE MIDST OF THIS HOLIEST OF RAGERS,
GOD SAT INTROVERTED IN THE CORNER OF INFINITY
FEELING ALONE & UNLOVED.

YOU SEE, THE ANGELS COULD NOT LOVE HIM FOR THEY

HAD NO CHOICE BUT TO. SO GOD CREATED THE EARTH

& SHE PROMISED TO DEVELOP LIFE THAT WOULD LOVE

HIM OF ITS OWN VOLITION. HE IGNITED THE SUN TO KEEP

HER WARM, MOLDED THE MOON SO SHE WOULD HAVE

SOMEONE TO HOLD. SHE STAYED TRUE TO HER WORD &

SOON PLANTS OF ALL SIZES & COLORS SPROUTED FROM
HER SKIN. BIRDS SOARED THROUGH HER WELCOMING
SKIES. HUMANS EXPLORED HER ANATOMY ON TWO FEET
& THEY ALL LOVED GOD—SO HE WAS HAPPY & SATISFIED.
UNTIL ONE DAY

EARTH & HER CHILDREN FORGOT ABOUT GOD. THEY

STARTED TO THINK THEMSELVES ALONE IN THE DARK

IMAGINATION OF SPACE. THEY TURNED TO SCIENCE

INSTEAD OF PRAYER. THEIR PHILOSOPHIES REPLACED THE

SCRIPTURES. THEIR ART SOOTHED THEIR LONELINESS

SO THEY FELT NO NEED FOR GOD. SOON MORALITY

CRUMBLED LIKE ROTTED WOOD. PRAYER WAS RIPPED OUT

SCHOOLS. CHURCHES WERE BOMBED & SHOT. MEN

FORNICATED WITH MEN, WOMEN FORNICATED WITH

WOMEN, & PASTORS WERE FORCED TO MARRY THEM WHEN

THEY FELL UNGRACEFULLY IN LOVE. FALSE PROPHETS

FORMED NEW RELIGIONS & THEIR FOLLOWERS GAVE

OTHER IDOLS THE LOVE THAT RIGHTFULLY BELONGED TO

HIM. & SO GOD, IN HIS RIGHTEOUS JUDGEMENT, DECIDED

HE WOULD PUNISH THOSE WHO REPAID HIS BLESSINGS

WITH BLASPHEME.

ONE NIGHT HE VISITED HIS MOST FAITHFUL,

THOSE DEVOUT CHRISTIANS WHO OBEYED HIS EVERY

COMMANDMENT, &   STOLE   THEM FROM THE

EARTH IN A HEAVENLY RAPTURE!

                    PILOTS VANISHED FROM COCKPITS.

AIRPLANES F
           E
            L
             L

          FROM THE SKY.

IF THE PLANE WAS FLOWN BY SINNERS,   GOD SMILED

& CLOUDS FLASHED

AS IF FOR A PICTURE   & IT WAS STRUCK BY

LIGHTNING.

HE LAUGHED A THUNDEROUS   B O O M

AS THOUSANDS   OF PASSENGERS PERISHED IN GLORIOUS

EXPLOSIONS.   & THIS WAS JUST HIS BEGINNING.

TRAINS   C   O   L   L I DED INTO STATIONS.

GOD

CAUGHT COMMUTERS IN HIS T E E T H   & HURLED THEM

B L O O D Y   THROUGH THE AIR.

THE SUN BURNED SAPPHIRE   & EARTH'S EVERY   BODY

OF WATER   WAS LEFT   A THIRSTY DITCH.

          GOD

                                        STOMPED

          A

                    JOYFUL

  DANCE

          & EARTHQUAKES

  RATTLED EVERY INCH OF EVERY CONTINENT.

                              STREETS CRA

CKED OPEN LIKE FOUL MOUTHS   & SWALLOWED

CITIES WHOLE.

THERE WAS NO PLACE FREE FROM HIS WRATH

OR THE SMELL OF BRIMSTONE

OR THE HAUNTING SCREAMS OF SOME DYING THING.

SURELY THEY CRIED OUT TO GOD TO SAVE THEM,

WOULDN'T YOU?

BUT HE WAS NO LONGER LISTENING.

HE REJOINED HIS PARTY IN PARADISE,

HAND IN HAND WITH HIS LOVERS,

& THEY LIVED HAPPILY EVER AFTER.

BUT TAKE HEED BELOVED.

THIS IS NO FANTASY OR WORK OF FICTION.

GOD IS COMING FOR YOU.

& FOR YOUR SAKE,

I PRAY HE LEAVES WITH YOU TOO. "

KINK.

you ever watch amateur porn
& fantasize about their friendship?
what? no? oh. same.

ROAST OF THE SOFT BOY.

after Airea D. Matthews

BOY   YOU SOFT.

WET NOODLE HAVING ASS NIGGA.

LIMBER TIMBER HAVING ASS NIGGA.

WHISKEY DICK WHEN SOBER ASS NIGGA.

"THIS HAS NEVER HAPPENED TO ME BEFORE"

WHEN THIS HAPPENS EVERY SINGLE TIME ASS NIGGA.

THUG IN THE STREETS

NEED A HUG IN THE SHEETS ASS NIGGA.

SCARED TO CUM TOO FAST

SO YOU DON'T CUM AT ALL ASS NIGGA.

BEDROOM STAGE FRIGHT HAVING ASS NIGGA.

I'M NOT A LOVER I'M A PERFORMER ASS NIGGA .

IMPOSTER DICKDROME HAVING ASS NIGGA.

RAP NAME "YOUNG IMPOTENCE" ASS NIGGA

MY ANACONDA

DON'T

WANT

NONE

UNLESS I FEEL COMFORTABLE ASS NIGGA

HIGH SEX-DRIVE LOW SELF-ESTEEM HAVING ASS NIGGA

ONLY THING YOU CAN TRUST IS JERGENS

IN YOUR RIGHT HAND ASS NIGGA

"CIALIS MIGHT BE FOR YOU" ASS NIGGA

SHAME GOT YOU BY THE SHAFT ASS NIGGA

NOT HARD ENOUGH ASS NIGGA

BOY   YOU SOFT.

HEY FELLAS, IS IT GAY?

to be born?   you're literally taking another man's genes.

to see colors?   you're always looking at a rainbow.

to make eye contact?   looking into another man's soul? that's suspect.

to shake hands?   hands touch dicks. transitive property.

to have cis-guy friends?   you're surrounding yourself with penises.

to visit a doctor?   another man telling *you* about *your* body?

to not be vegetarian?   you put meat in your mouth my guy???

to sleep?   hitting the sack? sounds p r e t t y gay to me.

to love Jesus?   you just gonna let another man save you?

to go to war?   fighting for another man? gaaaaaaaaaay.

to love yourself?   having deep affection for a man? *pause*.

to die?   maggots will eat your ass.

SELF-PORTRAIT AS MY DEAD FISH.

in my earliest memory / i see you. / stiff / on the cold floor. / lifeless blue / scales worn / like they just sliced clean / through a living room sky. / like they know home / is where whatever you're surviving / can't comfortably speak your name. /& i, too, am tired / of being loved by nowhere. / i fell / out my momma in 95' / & all i've owned since / is whatever oxygen / my lungs could thieve. / like you / i didn't ask to be here / but i'm tasked with living, / with swallowing / every flake of truth / my mistakes can conjure. / what i'm trying to say is— / i'm sorry. / i'm still learning / how to care / for a living thing. / everyone talks of healing / but no one describes / their healing / as the anguished fall / out of love / or the demolition / of a childhood / home / built on faulty concrete. / i know one day / i will also become / the flushed dead / circling the drain / of a loved one's memory. / still / i choose the slow suffocation / of what i know / over whatever freedom pools / outside the familiar. / & ain't that a poor origin / story for manhood? / ain't that enough / to make a boy / leap outside himself / & pray he lands / in a fresher body / of water?

SNAKE OIL GODS.

i was raised by God-fearing women
    who searched for men of God
        & found only men
            who thought themselves God.
                they say
                    men should be the head,
                    women should be the remains.
                if God wanted women to lead
            he would've made them first.
        yet every day i see women do the work
men claim to do without any of the praise.
        men want to be God
            but we don't even believe in ourselves.
                we know we're unworthy of faith
                    so we settle for unyielding fear.
                we want to be high & mighty
        so no one discovers how powerless we feel.
we lower self-expectations
        until the bar is in Hell,
            until any man on Earth
        can shine   like a god.

PATRILINEAGE.

the most selfless thing my grandfather ever did was stay.
one of two fathers on a crowded South Philly block.

for this act he will live forever, immortalized in my father's
longing & the stories he tells me of his childhood.

like the one where my grandfather teaches him to hold
his hands in fights against the neighborhood kids;

or when he pressed his palms into wet cement
just like in the movies they watched together.

my grandfather, a hero, for not abandoning his family.
revered for what he *didn't* do like only a man can be.

to this day my father never speaks of his father's violence.
how his father evicted him at 18. how he slept inside a car

until college brochures promised him shelter.
he discards these sour memories like orange rinds.

this is what it means to be a good son.
be grateful for a father even if he kills you.

my father's favorite defense
is that he never left us.

i don't know how to tell him
i wish he did.

for every tender moment
there are more still bleeding.

i disown him & he hisses
a father is a terrible thing to waste.

but most of my friends are fatherless.
some name this condition *misfortune*.

i stay silent to respect the shape of their wounds.
i've often been told i'm lucky to have had a father in the home

but the only time i knew how my father truly felt
was when he passed down the bruises his father left him.

he once told me i was the only one who understands him.
this must be what it means to be a bad son:

realize a present father is not present love.
see him as nothing more than a man.

FINE CHINA.

i learned to be a man
from the china cabinet
in my grandmother's home.

a porcelain patriarchy
housed in his wooden body.
my inheritance

behind his tall glass face
passed down for so long
it feels like he's always been there.

my grandmother says the fine china
is for special occasions.

this is one of her favorite lies.

there is never an occasion
that warrants him open
or vulnerable.

he is only there to impress guests.

the dining room his stage
he performs—stability.

every man i know is a performer.

more display than practice
or practicing some display
learned from other men.

my father tells me
boys don't cross their legs.
so i tell my brother the same.

i tell my friends
i've lost my virginity
& they tell me *it's about time.*

i've lied about my number of sexual partners
so often i forget the real amount.

i'm most manly when i forget.

my grandmother says   *boy you betta not run around my fine china!*
even she walks around him cautious.

how easily breaking
becomes another's burden.
fragile things take up the most space.

my father believes a man
should provide everything
for his family except an apology.

he taught me, women love persistence.
if you ask & she says   *no*
it's only because you haven't asked enough.

a woman taught me   rejection
& i gave her the resentment
that belonged to him.

when i ask my grandmother
where all of this came from.

she says
> *the gold-rimmed tea cups*
> *came from a mother.*

> *& their twin saucers*
> *also from a mother.*

> *& the egg-white plates*
> *painted with blue flowers*
> *from another mother.*

> *but we did not build the kiln*
> *that hardened you rigid boy.*

so i ask   what does a man leave behind?
& she says   nothing.

some nights, while my family sleeps
i imagine sneaking inside the dining room,

grabbing the cabinet by his neck
& throwing him to the floor.

he shatters.

i take off my father's shoes
& walk barefoot
through the glass.

with each step
i hear a crunch beneath
my feet that echoes his voice—

he says   *boys will be boys*

so i tell him
this is a mutiny of manhood.

i paint my nails bright colors
& cry for no reason.

he says   *boys don't cry*

so i sweat
& purge his poison.

i tell all my niggas i love them
& they say it back.

i sing a love song about a man
& don't change the pronouns.

he says   *pause*
so i move backwards.

rigor mortis before bitten dust.
breath before conception.

& i hear my grandmother's uncaged laughter.
her joints say there is just too much time in the day.

so we kick up our feet
& rest.

TRUE COLORS.

white people be like   *i don't see color.*
Black men be like   *it's all pink on the inside.*

Black women see red
& everybody be like

A WORD FROM OUR SPONSOR.

after Gabriel I. Green

tired of taking responsibility
for your actions?

want forgiveness without
any pesky remorse?

well then *Non-Apologies™*
just might be for you!

Non-Apologies™ works just like real apologies
except they keep your conscience nice & clean.

real apologies open deep psychological floodgates
suppressing immense sadness & self-loathing.

Non-Apologies™ don't cost you a thing
(if you don't count your integrity).

cheated on your partner? no problem!

Non-Apologies™ shifts the blame
so you can remain the victim.

caught being sexist in public? don't sweat it!

Non-Apologies^{TM} works especially well for men
as they're rarely expected to apologize anyway.

why live with the relentless weight of your mistakes
when with *Non-Apologies*^{TM} you can be an abuser in no time!

disclaimer: *Non-Apologies*^{TM} will damage your intimate relationships. side effects include: developing a sixth sense (a.k.a. "entitlement"); losing the respect of your peers; & stunting your growth as a functioning human adult. if you're not satisfied with your results, we're sorry you feel that way.

HOUSE OF MIRRORS.

as boys i scolded my
brother for buying a
fake id but to this day
i carry a false identity
everywhere i go.

my father & i could
be good friends but
he will never own the
blood on his hands.

i stay quiet in the
face of misogyny
& hope silence
buys me the dull
edge of the scythe.

my mother can
locate anything
i've lost but she
can't help me
find myself.

i'm so accustomed to
privilege that equity
feels like injustice.

whatever i have to
lose by speaking
against hate never
belonged to me
but i still feel
entitled to it.

i'm a stranger to
myself. all my life
people have told
me who i am.

as a child i
pulled covers
over my head
when i heard
momma's
body hit
the floor
& i never
came out of
hiding. the
truth doesn't
drag me out
of bed.

i wouldn't
know intimacy
if it was my
mother.

my respect for women
only stretches as far as the
shadow of my family tree.

i think love &
domination eat
at the same table.

i know sexuality isn't
a choice because why
else would someone
want me?

i've mastered
the art of
emotional self-
mutilation
so well i don't
even realize
i'm bleeding
out.

i was promised
dominion & all i got
was depression.

i was raised a boy,
endowed a rain cloud for
a crown. & like all sons, i
rose in search of daylight
& found only deluge.

i'm a revolving door
for emotions i've
been conditioned to
suppress.

i'm a bruise-
colored
highway
whose cost
each lover an
emotional toll.

Enoch says *any man can fall*. i pray the same goes for those willing to rise.

i have the privilege to be judged by how much i've grown, not by what my growth has cost those who grew me.

an apology is only worth its weight in reparation.

real power comes at no one's expense.

i will never be free until every Black queer disabled trans person is free.

the reward for hard work is more hard work. some days my best isn't enough.

some days there is pain & no one to blame.

when the dust settles, i will have nothing but what love has forged from my fear.

unlearning is not a destination, its daily practice.

RESURRECTION.

in the garden of Gethsemane,
Jesus Christus   begged God
not to let him be crucified.

he wanted to live
but God needed him dead
so he died   *a savior.*

i was raised to be like Christ.
a faithful servant. a willing participant
in my own destruction.

i was never taught to protect myself,
say   *no*
or prioritize my needs.

now i am an insecure god,
jealous & self-loathing,
demanding sacrifice

but only loving myself
as burnt offering.

what i mean is—

i am the martyr & the cause.
the crucifixion & the bloodlust
that names itself redemption.

my love language is self-sacrifice
every relationship   an altar
i leave each one emptier than before.

if Jesus knew he would be killed
but still willed himself nailed to a cross
is he savior   or suicidal?

if i killed myself
they would call it
tragedy

but i die a little every day
& they call me
the strong friend.

if it were me in Gethsemane,
i would probably follow Christ
& be tortured for the need

of all humanity out of guilt
or fear of disappointing my father.
but i can imagine another me

who is confident & honest,
who tells God   *nah*.
i am no one's salvation.

i am
what i am
& that is good enough.

my self-esteem is so high
my demons get vertigo.

i am not the strong friend
but i am still worth
being checked on.

i don't deserve to suffer.

there is an exit sign
over every stage of grief.

i won't die for anyone's cause.
i am a cause worth living for.

A CHURCH OF MY OWN.

Sunday shoes, unfilled
pews on Saturday,
everyday is Saturday
in this church of my own.

pews on Saturday,
rows of empty ribs
in this church of my own
which is also a body.

rows of empty ribs
starving themselves
which is also a body
unfamiliar with living.

starving themselves
if daily bread is faith
unfamiliar with living
let the church say, *amen*.

if daily bread is faith
family eats their fill,
let the church say, *amen*
i am all that is leftover.

family eats their fill
still growing into church,
i am all that is leftover
smiling from outside.

still growing into church,
everyday is Saturday
smiling from outside,
Sunday shoes, unfilled.

SOMNILOQUIES.

i.
i'm standing inside a burning home surrounded by endless smoke
midnight Black & rising like an Angelou poem & my tongue is a fire
hose but i say   nothing   because it's not my house

ii.
i'm in the roaring heart of a BLM protest spilling over the city streets like
milk or Black blood or whatever else they say ain't worth crying over but
i'm late for a dick appointment so i run away without realizing the boy on
their posters is me

iii.
i arrive at the interview for a job that earns my mother's comfort
i wipe my ghetto at the front door of a boss who names it *unprofessional*
i switch my tongue for one less jagged & lose the original
i wake & never find out if they hire me

iv.
i'm up all night studying for the most important exam of my life
i watch the clumsy sun leak a new dawn through my window
i realize the exam was cancelled
i know all the answers to a test i'll never take

v.
i put a gun to my head   pull the trigger   & all that comes out
is a really long poem.

REVELATION.

i know God isn't a man
because God knows everything
& never says   *well, actually...*

ELEGY FOR JIMMY.

there was a time when i wanted you dead.

only God knows if you deserved to leave us without answers or apologies but maybe God knew we'd never get them.

your wife gave you everything & you left her empty. did you know she told me she couldn't be free until you were gone? i prayed for your departure like the end to a tireless war.

your grave is my father's open wound. did you know he asked me to never let him become like you? i look like my father & my father looks like you. but your father was faceless. so you never knew how it felt to stare in the mirror & see someone you don't want to become.

you gave me what you thought i needed. but all i ever wanted was the man under the church robes—███████ my first hero. your love so scarce it became valuable.

remember when you came to my football game? you watched me warm a bench for hours but when you said you were proud of me the gratification warmed my heart for years.

i started writing these words the last time i saw light in your eyes. your shriveled palm in mine while i typed everything i didn't have the courage to name.

i wish i knew you better than the scars you made. your pain memorialized in the silence your children cling to like a precious heirloom.

i no longer believe in the Heaven you preached. but i do believe in the dirt we planted you in. maybe it's the first thing since your momma to hold you & not be afraid.

when i said i wouldn't cry at your funeral. i lied. i never really wanted you dead. only to feel your hand & not flinch.

BIRTHDAY WISHES (III).

/alternate ending/

in her final moments   A█████   loses the strength to cry
so she prays   as her temperature climbs   like Moses up Mt. Sinai
until suddenly—   she ignites   our four-door Ford
engulfs in hallowed flame,   melts into chariot   & takes off
soaring over the Philly skyline.   maybe you saw her that night
& thought her a star   shooting towards Heaven.   maybe your ears
caught the trail   of her laughter, popping   like loose fireworks.
maybe you just had to be there.   my birthday,   an inside joke
told in God's perfect comedic timing.   now   there is no earthly
trace of A█████   left.   about her disappearance,   there were
no reporters called   or articles   written with sore eyes;
no one to arrest or shop for caskets   in sizes   you'd rather forget exist.
instead, my family   wakes   & we throw our bodies
in euphoric dance,   a lively grief   expressed in stomps,
shouts & *Hallelujah!*   as our A███smiles on us   full of pity,
knowing   what it means to be trapped;   freed   from the
fear   of being forgotten.

73

INSECTICIDE.

after Nikki Giovanni

i'm most my mother's son
when killing bugs
on her behalf.

she wages war
on every invading creature
but refuses to dirty her hands.

this is why i have sons
she sighs
as i loom over the damned

wielding some object
that would be harmless
in another's grip:

a flimsy tissue;
today's depressing newspaper;
a ragged boot i can swing like a curse.

anything becomes a weapon
with the wrong intention.

how powerful i feel imposed
over a defenseless thing.

the most dangerous part
of being a man is no one questions
your capacity for ruin.

i was born an executioner.
a stoic soldier primed
for ungraceful work.

when i was a boy my mother said
the man of the house
is a ruthless protector

so i slept with knives
beneath my pillow
like baby teeth.

i didn't believe in the tooth fairy
but i knew violence certain
like taxes

& i paid my dues
to the fraternity
of blood.

                                        crushed every unlucky pest
                              mistaking some forgettable corner
                                          of our home for refuge.

the real tragedy is that
now i'm nonviolent

                                        but afraid to be loved less
                                              if i'm not violent.

if the fear my hands can inspire
is only ever hypothetical

                                              i'm not the man
                                           i was raised to be.

when my sister introduces me
to her boyfriends it will be my duty

                        to grill them like drunk uncles at cookouts.
                              this is my side of the bargain:

i want my loved ones to feel protected
but i don't know if i can protect them.

raise a boy
to be something he can never be
& he'll spend his entire life pretending

the ceiling over his head isn't falling
stark & heavy   like the bottom
of a shoe.

CAUGHT UP IN THE LIE.

if
  you
    don't
      know
        what
          you
            have
              until
                it's
                  gone
                    what
                      a
                        curse
                            to
                              lose
                              something
                              precious
                            &
                              never
                              learn
                                it's
                              value.

i'm 15 clutching the .44 magnum
in my grandfather's night stand.

he thinks his bedside safe
from the curious hands of a child

but underestimates how gravely
i want to feel dangerous.

i don't even know if it's loaded.
maybe it's just as empty i feel.

i'm supposed to be bulletproof.
been told to *man up* so often

i hate everything about myself
that doesn't resemble a weapon.

but in this moment, i'm lethal.
i'm everything expected of me.

i take aim at everyone
who ever made me feel like dying.

first ▮▮▮▮, who gives back the money
he bullied out of me the week before.

then ▮▮▮ who recants every threat
that ever slipped off his tongue in my direction.

then ▮▮▮▮, who doesn't talk shit
on the bus now that i have the power

to make his grandmother question
the efficacy of her prayers.

then myself, my favorite target.
i stare into my warped reflection

on the revolver's steel body
& wonder if i'm man enough to die.

my father wanted to be a singer
& settled for a patriarch,
as a boy, he sang
like the world rested
in his throat
now
all that lives there
is a resentment born
when he became the man
his father wanted him to be.

a thief is anyone
who ignores a boundary.
even if the boundary is memory.
even if the thief has also been robbed.
i was born into a crime scene.
my father pleads the fifth

to his abuses but takes credit
for everything else in my life.
my mother puts me through school,
he says *i picked the right woman*.
i graduate through sheer perseverance,
he says *my cruelty made you strong*.
it seems all he won't take
responsibility for is the trauma.

i nurture this grudge against him
better than he does any of his children.
there are days my unforgiveness
feels like his getaway car.
i gamble my happiness
on his willingness to confess
& lose every single time.
it's the perfect crime.

i have no language for anxiety / but i'm fluent in anger— / the disoriented
emotion. / always needing direction. / i fear who it might make me / so
i swallow it. / play the nice guy. / so nice / i'll only hurt you by accident.
/ there is harm / on all sides of expression. / i'm a rifle firing inwards. /
pretending / i won't eventually / ricochet into casualty. / pretending / i'm
not already casualty. / far too often / my anger / is not where it should be. /
i misplace my rage / like car keys.

in arguments / i don't reach for understanding. / peace is not as valuable
to me / as being correct. / all my life i've been right. / i don't know how to
be wrong. / all my life i've felt like an object / so that's what i create / out
of everyone around me. / i'm addicted / to friction. / to the righteousness
/ that shadows my indignation. / the days i have no enemy / are the most
difficult / to survive.

this morning / i drove to work / & honked at the world's slowest bus. /
i imagine / it filled with 30 passengers / going to 30 destinations / for 30
distinct reasons. / but i lay on my horn / cause none of them are me.

CREDITS.

thank you to the following publications for publishing (in some form) the following poems from this book:

- ♥ "genesis." - Wusgood Magazine
- ♥ "the show must go on." - International Human Rights Art Festival
- ♥ "fine china." - ARTS x SDGS, Motion Pictures International Film Festival, Midwest Video Poetry Fest, Monologues & Poetry International Film Fest, International Film Festival of Thuringia.
- ♥ "self-portrait as my dead fish." - Quaranzine: Art in Isolation

how my memory is set up i can barely remember what i ate for breakfast this morning let alone every person who deserves credit for this manuscripts existence so sorry in advance if i miss some folks!

first, i gotta thank God. my God. & my momma for believing in me & always encouraging me to pursue my passions. & my father for everything you've taught me. & my sister for allowing me to solicit your opinions, & my brother for helping me keep things in perspective. & Bj for your loyalty & friendship. & all of SKG (*stand up!*), especially my aunties & Brandon for being honest with me & supporting my career however you could.

& Davon for inspiring me to write about what i love & never letting me forget to relax. & Rabiyatu for always having my back. & Kai & Jasmine for letting me crash on your couch Odunde 2018 & giving me space to be myself. & Miriam for just being a real nigga & for coming up with the name for this book. & Shanel for giving me permission to be tender. & Nayo for giving me permission to be myself.

& Sanam for being my sibling in thoughtfulness. & Mateo for always checking in on me. & Rodrick for always looking out. & Jamal & Mike & Pratt for being inspirations & always giving me good energy. & Talia for being a good friend & supporting my love for Cracker Barrel. & Jacob for showing love & sharing opportunities. & Kirwyn for mentoring & affirming me. & Enoch for being one of the most authentic niggas i know & creating a platform that gives Black poets the freedom to realize their dreams.

& New Consolation, the village who raised me. & W.O.R.D.S. & everyone whose lives it linked to mine, especially Millie for providing & protecting me. & Gabe for constantly challenging me to be a better writer & person.

& the tribe i made through CUPSI, IWPS, NPS & The Watering Hole. & all the teachers who encouraged my love of language: Ms. Minges who introduced me to *The House on Mango Street*, Mogg who showed me that writing should be fun, & Camille who read early drafts of this book.

& bell hooks, & Audre Lorde, & James Baldwin, & Danez Smith, & Hanif Abdurraqib, & Rasheed Copeland, & Kirwyn Sutherland (again), & Julian Randall, & Jericho Brown, & Dave Harris, & Raych Jackson for putting your work into the world & inadvertently giving me the blueprint for this manuscript.

& every Black feminist who made/makes it possible for "soft boys" to exist out loud. everything i've said in this book has already been said more eloquently & effectively by queer disabled Black women & trans activists who birthed & drive the Black liberation movement.

& lastly, thank you afaq. for everything. the trust. the grace. the advice. the edits. the laughs. the culture. the new experiences. for helping me want more for myself. you make me feel beautiful & i will always love you for that. you gave me a safe space to take the mask off even when i didn't deserve it. you held me down more than my weighted blanket. this book wouldn't exist without you. i wouldn't be who i am without you. & for that all i can say is thank you. thank you. thank you.

until next time,
Dave G

ABOUT THE AUTHOR.

David A. Gaines (Dave G) is a Black poet, actor & filmmaker born
& raised in the greater Philadelphia area. He is a champion of the
College Unions Poetry Slam Invitational, the Fuze Poetry Slam, the
Philly Pigeon, & ranked 4th in the nation in the 2018 Individual
World Poetry Slam. In 2020, Dave's poetry film, "fine china.", received
international acclaim & he was awarded the title Poet Laureate of
Pennsylvania's Montgomery County. He has been featured in the
National Black Arts Festival, International Human Rights Art Festival,
Wusgood Magazine, Write About Now, VICE Media, among many
others. He also loves yo-yos & is a connoisseur of pickles.

www.davegpoetry.com   Twitter & Instagram: @davegpoetry

ABOUT BLACK MINDS PUBLISHING.

Black Minds Publishing is a national publications platform centered around the personal and professional growth of artists and creatives of the Black diaspora. At Black Minds Publishing we aim to give more visibility to raw artistic works, both literary and visual, that center on the healing process of the Black mind, body and spirit. We aren't concerned with the rigid expectations of academia or the "supposed to's" of artistic gatekeepers and instead choose to prioritize genuine works that have meaningful impact for its readers.

ALSO BY BLACK MINDS PUBLISHING.

Burned at the Roots by Enoch the Poet

Journal Entry by Jovan McKoy

BE by LindoYes

Made in the USA
Monee, IL
18 March 2021